Seeing Light and Dark

Written by
Jill Atkins

Marcus cannot see well.

He had a test at the clinic.

All he can see is light and dark, but he can still do lots of things.

He can go swimming with his mum and his sister.

He might win the cup for the best swimmer.

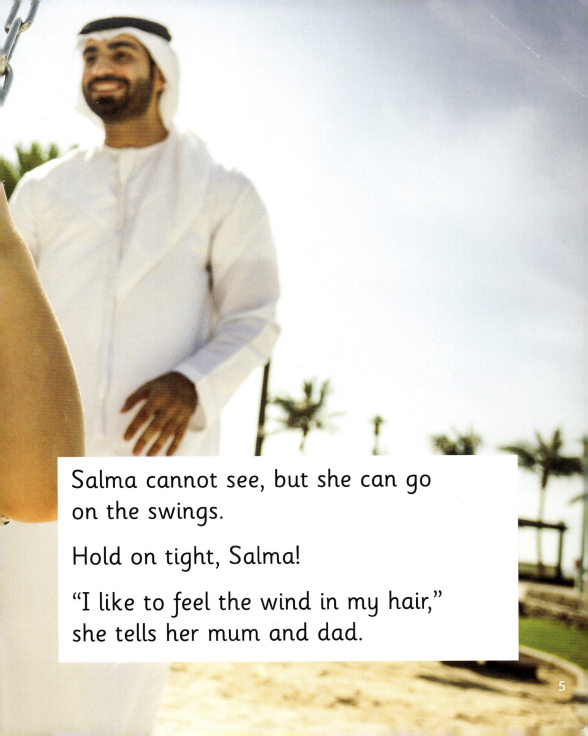

Salma cannot see, but she can go on the swings.

Hold on tight, Salma!

"I like to feel the wind in my hair," she tells her mum and dad.

When Tom and Jordan go out, Tom can "see" with his ears.

Jordan tells him that bats click to help them "see", but Tom is not a bat!

In the street Tom hears
"Cheep cheep!"

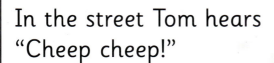

"Vroom, vroom!"

"Clip clop!"

"Chatter chatter!"

"Ding ding!"

Jordan tells him what things look like.

When Tom hears "Beep beep!" at the crossing, that tells him he and Jordan can cross the road.

In the street, this man can "see" with his feet.

He can tell if it is smooth or if he is going up or down hill.

His feet tell him if he is on the bumps. His stick can help him if there are steps.

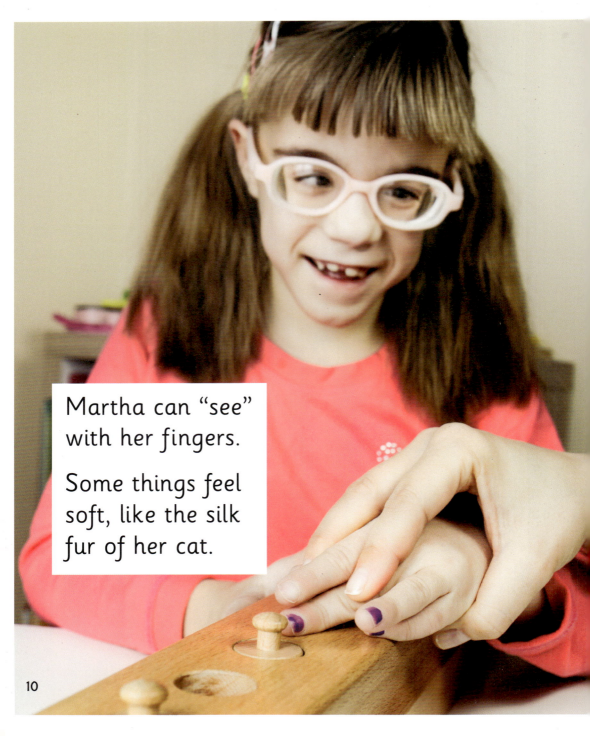

Martha can "see" with her fingers.

Some things feel soft, like the silk fur of her cat.

Some things feel sharp and some are cold.

She can feel the hard pegs under her fingers. Her hands tell her what they "look" like.

When Hannah's mum or dad cook dinner, she can smell what they are cooking.

So she can tell what is for dinner without needing to see.

She is fond of the smell of lemons, flowers and lavender, but she is not fond of the smell of petrol or poo!
They stink!

"When I am bigger I will do lots of things," Callum tells us.

"I will do some sports on the back of a tandem. We will speed along!"

"I might run a marathon with a helper," Jack tells us.

"But best of all, I will have a Seeing Dog," Kasim tells us.

"It will be so clever it will help me go to the shops or on a train. I will have a dog like this one. They are the best."